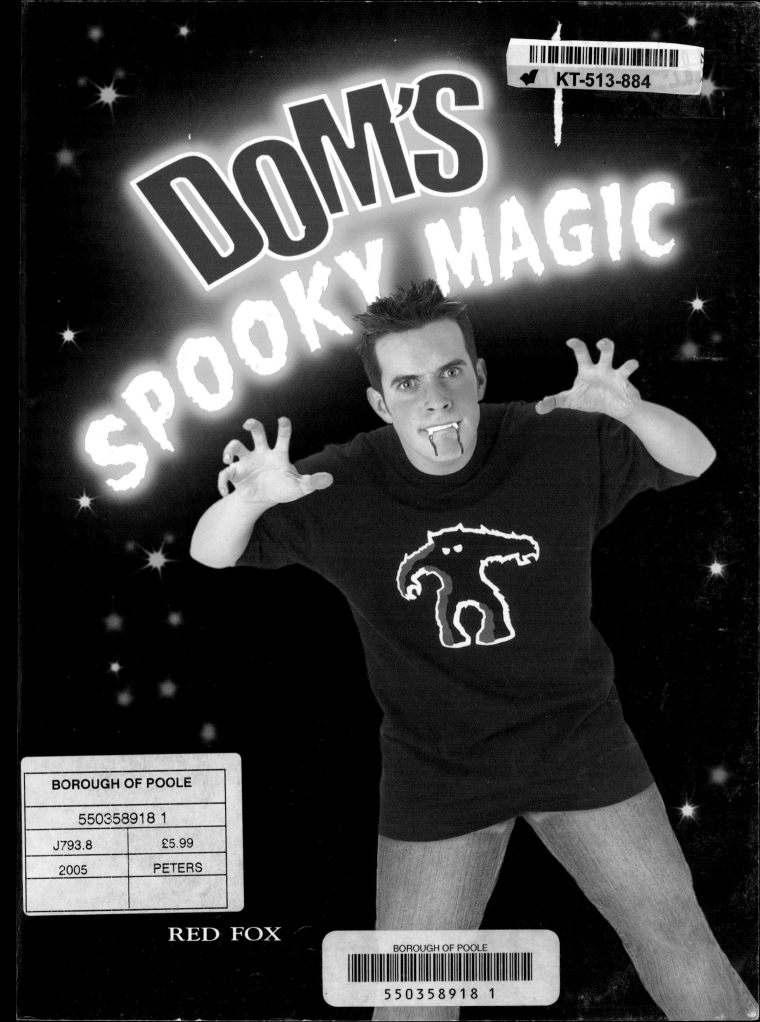

DOM'S SPOOKY MAGIC

RED FOX

To my mum and dad

DOM'S SPOOKY MAGIC
A RED FOX BOOK 0 099 44768 1

First published in Great Britain by The Bodley Head,
an imprint of Random House Children's Books

The Bodley Head edition published 2003
Red Fox edition published 2005

1 3 5 7 9 10 8 6 4 2

Text copyright © Dominic Wood, 2003

With thanks to Mark Leveridge, photographer Roddy Paine and models Christian Perera-Slater,
Paul and Cherie Constable, Edith Cockrell, Paisley Thomas, Gemma Banfield, Lily Francis and Nat Paine

The right of Dominic Wood to be identified as the author of this work has been
asserted in accordance with the Copyright, Designs and Patents Act 1988.

Red Fox Books are published by Random House Children's Books,
61–63 Uxbridge Road, London W5 5SA,
a division of The Random House Group Ltd,
in Australia by Random House Australia (Pty) Ltd,
20 Alfred Street, Milsons Point, Sydney, NSW 2061, Australia,
in New Zealand by Random House New Zealand Ltd,
18 Poland Road, Glenfield, Auckland 10, New Zealand,
and in South Africa by Random House (Pty) Ltd,
Endulini, 5A Jubilee Road, Parktown 2193, South Africa

THE RANDOM HOUSE GROUP Limited Reg. No. 954009
www.kidsatrandomhouse.co.uk
www.dominicwood.co.uk

A CIP catalogue record for this book is available from the British Library.

Printed in China

Check out the star rating to see how difficult the trick is to learn or perform:

★☆☆☆☆   easy

★★☆☆☆   moderate

★★★☆☆   difficult

★★★★☆   very difficult

★★★★★   extremely difficult

You can master all the tricks in this book with practice!

CONTENTS

INTRODUCTION

BOO! Ha, just kidding. Welcome to my brand new magic book. You know what, a few months ago I was in the attic of my house practising all my magic tricks and I noticed that quite a lot of them were really spooky. That gave me the idea to invent some creepy and incredible tricks so that you guys could shock your friends! Some tricks have a haunted and eerie feel, like 'Napkin Spirits' on page 26, where a shape appears under a napkin. Others are just plain terrifying, like 'Dead Man's Finger' on page 32. But they are all perfect for scaring your little brother or sister! I had such a laugh with these tricks and I know you will too.

HAPPY SPOOKING!

Dominic Wood

THE ART OF DISTRACTION

Make sure your audience does not discover your magic secrets by distracting them during your tricks!

TALK TO YOUR AUDIENCE

While you perform your tricks try to be funny and interesting, or make up a story about the trick you are performing. If you give your audience something to think about or laugh at they will not watch you so closely.

WATCH WHERE YOU LOOK

Spectators look where you look, so do not look at anything you do not want your audience to notice. For example, if you pretend to put something in your pocket but really keep it in your hand, look at a prop in front of you and your audience will do the same.

LOOK NATURAL

Many tricks involve hiding a prop in your hand. When you do this, try to make sure that your hand looks natural, not stiff. If you look relaxed people will not notice that you have something hidden.

KEEP THE SPECTATOR BUSY

Break someone's concentration by making them do something for you. Ask them to examine a prop or give you an object from the table. This will keep them busy while you weave your magic!

WATCH WHAT YOU SAY

Do not draw too much attention to the objects you use in your tricks. It is better to ask someone to examine a prop than to say, 'I have here an ordinary box,' as this may make people wonder if it really *is* ordinary!

Good luck!

Dress to Impress

For a really spooky performance wow your audience with a creepy costume!

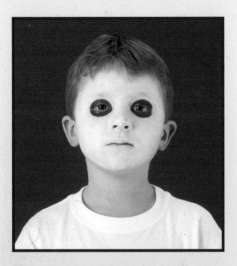

WHAT YOU NEED TO BECOME A MUMMY
- White T-Shirt
- White, black and red face paints
- Lots of bandages!

1 Put on the T-shirt and ask someone to paint your face white with red circles covering your eye sockets.

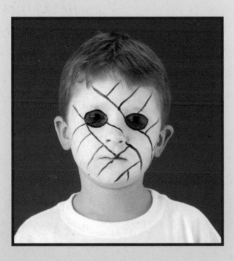

2 Use a thin brush to paint black lines around the red eye sockets. Then draw more lines across your face to look like bandages.

3 Colour your lips dark red in a thin line. Now close your eyes and ask a helper to draw creepy black eyes on your eyelids.

4 Now your helper can wrap you in the bandages. Ask them to start with your head and work down your body. If you have enough bandages let some hang loosely around your arms – this will make you look like a mummy that's just woken up from the dead!

You can try all sorts of spooky costumes – how about a vampire or a witch?

To be a vampire paint your face white with dark eyes and eyebrows and red lips. Then paint on two white fangs at the edge of your mouth and add some red to show them dripping with blood! Gel your hair down and wear a white shirt and bow tie. A black cape will finish it off – now you can go out hunting!

To be a witch paint your face white with red eyes and lips. Add some wrinkles, spiky eyebrows and cobweb lines on your cheeks. To finish your face you need one or two big black warts! For the rest of your costume wear a black cloak and a witch's hat.

★ STAR TIPS ★

To make a witch's hat use black card to make a cone (like in 'Wizards' Hats' on page 38, but bigger). It should fit on your head but be a bit too big. Cut into the bottom of the hat several times to make tabs. Fold these back so that the hat fits perfectly. Cut two big circles of card with a hole in the middle big enough to fit over the cone. Slide one circle over the cone and stick it to the tabs with glue or tape. Then stick the other circle to the bottom of the hat to cover up the tabs.

...oulish Glasses

...nster, a vampire and a witch turn clear water green, red and black!

PREPARATION

1. Put a drop of the green food colouring in one of the glasses, a drop of the red food colouring in another, and a drop of the black food colouring in the last.

2. Place the glasses and the jug of water on a table and put the food colouring out of sight.

PERFORMANCE

1. Explain to the audience that the three glasses each belong to a different ghoul. Tell them that the glasses have taken on the mark of their evil owners!

2. Pour a little water into each glass – it will turn a different colour each time.

3. Tell the audience that the green glass belongs to the slime monster, the black glass belongs to the witch, and the red glass belongs to the vampire!

COOKIE MONSTER

An invisible monster takes a bite out of a biscuit!

WHAT YOU NEED
- Some biscuits
- A dessert bowl

PREPARATION

1 Take a bite out of one of the biscuits.

2 Tip the rest of the biscuits into the bowl and hide the bitten biscuit under some of the others so that no one can see the bitten side, but so you know where it is.

PERFORMANCE

1 Show the bowl of biscuits and hand out one or two of them to your audience, making sure you do not give away the bitten biscuit, or any of the biscuits covering it.

2 Reach into your pocket with your left hand and bring it out cupped as if you are holding something. Tell the audience you have an invisible cookie monster in your hand – who loves eating cookies!

3 Reach into the bowl with your right hand and pick up the bitten biscuit so that your fingers cover the bite hole.

4 Place the biscuit in your left hand and pretend to watch the monster eating the biscuit for a moment. Then show the bite hole in the biscuit to the audience and tell them that the monster has eaten a chunk right out of it!

SPIDER SENSE

A magician uses his powers to find the hidden creepy crawly!

WHAT YOU NEED
- Five identical, empty matchboxes
- A pen
- A small plastic spider

PREPARATION

I Take one of the matchboxes and put a very small dot on the top with the pen. Make sure it is clear to you, but not obvious to anyone else.

PERFORMANCE

I Place the matchboxes on a table in a row. Show the spider to your audience, drop it into the marked matchbox and close it up.

2 Ask a member of the audience to mix up the boxes while you turn away.

3 Turn round and spot the box with the dot on the top. Open it up to reveal the spider inside!

★ STAR TIPS ★
When you look for the box with the dot on top try not to be too obvious. Distract your audience by telling them that you are about to use your spider supersense!

Funny Bones

Some broken bones magically join back together into a spooky skeleton!

WHAT YOU NEED
- Two large, brown envelopes
- Scissors
- Two identical skeleton pictures

PREPARATION

1 Cut out one whole side of an envelope and slip it inside the other to create a secret compartment.

2 Cut up one of the pictures so the skeleton is in pieces. Put these into the front compartment of the envelope. Put the other, complete picture of the skeleton into the back compartment.

PERFORMANCE

1 Open the envelope to show the front compartment and shake out the cut-up skeleton pieces. The envelope will now appear empty.

2 Explain that it would take ages to put the bones back together to make a skeleton, but you can use your magic to do it in seconds!

3 Drop the pieces back into the front compartment of the envelope and close the flap. Say a few magic words, open it up again and reach into the *back* compartment. Slide out the complete skeleton. Show the 'empty' envelope to the audience and they will be amazed!

The Mummies' Curse

The bandages belonging to three mummies behave in extraordinary ways.

PREPARATION

WHAT YOU NEED
- A4 paper
- Scissors
- Sticky tape

1 Take two sheets of paper and cut them lengthways into three equal strips each. Stick two strips together end to end to make one long strip. Do the same with the others so that you end up with three long strips.

★ **STAR TIPS** ★
If you have time it is better to use glue to stick the paper strips together.

2 Take one strip and stick the ends together to make a loop. Take another and twist the paper once before sticking the ends together. Take the last strip and twist the paper twice before sticking the ends together.

PERFORMANCE

1 Show the loops to the audience and tell them that they are bandages taken from three Egyptian mummies.

2 Take the first loop with no twists and cut it in two down its length. When you get all the way round it will separate into two loops – tell the audience that this bandage comes from a mummy who cut his victim's limbs in two!

3 Cut the second loop, with one twist, in the same way. You will end up with one large loop. This bandage comes from the mummy who stretched his victims to twice their normal height!

4 Cut the last loop, with two twists, and you will end up with two loops linked together. This bandage comes from the mummy who kept his victim chained up for all eternity!

Spirit Message

A blank piece of paper sealed inside a matchbox emerges with a message from the spirit world!

PREPARATION

WHAT YOU NEED
- A small pad of thick, or dark, paper
- A pencil stub
- A large, empty matchbox

1 Remove any cardboard from the pad of paper so that it looks the same whichever way up it is held.

PERFORMANCE

2 On the last page of the pad write an eerie message with the pencil stub.

1 Hold the pad with the message sheet at the bottom. Flick through the pages casually to show that they are blank. But do not let the last page with the writing show!

2 Turn the pad over and place it on the table. Then open the matchbox and put the pencil stub inside.

3 Take the top sheet of paper from the pad, making sure that no one sees the writing on it. Fold it several times so that the writing is hidden, then drop it into the matchbox and close the box.

4 Explain to the audience that spirits from the other realm will enter the matchbox and use the pencil to write a message on the blank paper.

5 After a few moments open the matchbox, take out the paper and reveal the spooky message!

★ **STAR TIPS** ★
This can be really spooky if you play up the part of the spirit world. Write something you know about a member of the audience, like 'Daniel's afraid of the dark . . . and he should be!'

Spooky Spider

A spider seeks out an envelope containing its name – it's uncanny!

WHAT YOU NEED
- Seven blank pieces of card
- A pen
- Four small envelopes
- A small, plastic spider

PREPARATION

1 Write the word 'spider' on four of the cards and put one of these 'spider' cards into three of the envelopes.

PERFORMANCE

1 Show the audience the four cards that are left – three blank cards and one 'spider' card – and tell the audience that you have four empty envelopes. Then pick up the one truly empty envelope and show the inside to the audience.

3 Close all the envelopes and ask a member of the audience to mix them up and lay them out in a row. Hand the spider to your helper and ask them to pass it over the envelopes before placing it on top of one of them.

2 Pick up the last 'spider' card and slip it into the empty envelope. Then pick up the other envelopes and slip a blank card into each one, making sure that it goes in front of the 'spider' card already inside.

4 Pick up the chosen envelope and take out the card at the back. The spider has magically chosen the envelope containing the word 'spider'!

★ **STAR TIPS** ★
You do not have to use a spider for this trick. A plastic skull or anything creepy will work just as well.

Magic Monsters

There's a monster on the loose, but you can track it down with your monster magic!

WHAT YOU NEED
- Seven blank pieces of card
- A pen
- A piece of paper

PREPARATION

1 On each card draw a different monster – e.g. a vampire, werewolf, mummy, etc. Choose your favourite – werewolf, for instance – and write that name on the piece of paper. Fold it in half to hide your prediction.

PERFORMANCE

1 Place the cards face up on a table so that your audience can see them. Explain that one of these monsters is on the loose and you are going to track it down.

2 Tell the audience you already know which monster it will be. Hold up your folded paper and say that you have written down the name of the escaped monster. Place the folded paper on the table where everyone can see it.

3 Turn all the cards over and, remembering which one is the werewolf, mix them up on the table, keeping track of the werewolf.

4 Pick up any card except the werewolf and place it face down in your left hand. Then pick up the werewolf and put it face down on top of the first. Continue collecting the other cards and add them to the pile in your hand in any order.

5 Hand the pile to a member of the audience, keeping it face down and tell them to place the first card on the table, then the next card at the bottom of the pile in their hand. The next card goes on the table, and the card after that goes to the bottom of the pile in their hand until there is only one card left.

★ **STAR TIPS** ★
When you pick up the cards, casually tell the audience that you will make a pile by picking up the cards in a random order.

6 Take this card and turn it over to reveal the werewolf. Now show your prediction to the audience – they will be amazed!

Strange Straw

An ordinary straw moves across a table . . .
without the magician touching it!

WHAT YOU NEED
• A plastic drinking straw

PERFORMANCE

1 Lay the straw on the table top and tell the audience you can move the straw without touching it.

2 Lean over so that your head is close to the straw and hold your hand out flat over the straw with your palm facing down.

3 Tell the audience to look very carefully at the straw as you use your powers to move it. Then slowly move your hand away from you across the table and at the same time quietly blow at the straw. It will move spookily on its own!

★ STAR TIPS ★
Practise this in front of a mirror to check that you do not look as if you are blowing and try to time it so that your hand moves with the straw. This trick works best on a shiny table top.

GHOSTLY THREAD

A handkerchief is tugged by invisible thread – you can see it moving, but you cannot see how!

WHAT YOU NEED
• A handkerchief

PERFORMANCE

2 Pretend to pick up an invisible thread and sew it through the top of the handkerchief, telling the audience what you are doing.

I Pick up the handkerchief by the middle and hold it in your left hand so that the middle pokes up above your hand, and your left thumb is behind the handkerchief, facing you.

3 Tell the audience that they may not be able to see the thread, but you can prove it is there by tugging it. Pretend to pull the thread away from you with your right hand. At the same time push your left thumb into the handkerchief. The top of the handkerchief will jerk forward as if the thread is tugging it!

★ **STAR TIPS** ★
This is a great trick that looks fabulous with a bit of practice. Try it in front of a mirror to make sure it looks really good.

Poisoned Chalice

You avoid the poisoned chalice, but your spectator chooses it every time!

WHAT YOU NEED
- Eight identical containers
- A pen
- A piece of paper

PERFORMANCE

PREPARATION

1 Put a small mark on one of the containers so that you can spot it, but no one else will. Write the word 'Poison' on the piece of paper and close it up inside the marked container.

1 Place the eight containers on a table saying that one of them contains poison. Ask a spectator to mix up the containers behind your back and arrange them in a row.

2 Turn round, spot the marked container and tell your helper that you will both eliminate the pots until one of you is left with the poisoned chalice.

3 Ask your helper to point to two containers. Then remove one of these, making sure you do not choose the marked container. Next you point to two containers, making sure you do not point to the marked one, and your helper chooses which one to remove.

4 Repeat step 3 until two containers are left. It will be your turn to choose which one to remove so pick the last unmarked container and ask your helper to open theirs to reveal the poison.

Ghostly Game

A board game starts to float up and down mysteriously!

PREPARATION

PERFORMANCE

1 Using the hairbands, strap the ruler to the underside of your right arm. Make sure that they hold the ruler firmly in place, but that they are not tight or uncomfortable.

2 Make sure that the end of the ruler reaches past your palm a little. Hide the ruler with the sleeve of your jumper.

1 Place the board game on a table and slide it towards you with your left hand. Hold it steady while you slide the ruler under the edge of the board with your right arm.

2 Move both your hands so that they are in the middle of the board and start to wiggle your fingers and raise up your arms a little. The edge of the board will be lifted up by the ruler underneath.

★ **STAR TIPS** ★
You can do this trick whenever you play a board game if you prepare in secret first.

3 Raise and lower your arms a few times, making sure you do not lift the board too high. It will look as though the board is rising up and down on its own!

napkin spirits

Ghostly spirits slip under a napkin to spook the audience!

WHAT YOU NEED
- A fork
- A small, cloth napkin

PREPARATION

1 Sit at a table with the fork lying in your lap, prongs towards you and facing up. Cover it with the napkin.

PERFORMANCE

1 Pick up the napkin with both hands and use your thumb to secretly hold the fork at the same time.

2 Carefully lay the napkin on the table so that the fork is secretly hidden underneath it. Use your thumb to aim the handle end of the fork towards the centre of the napkin.

3 Tell your audience that there are spirits about and you will call them under the napkin. Slowly press down the prongs of the fork a few times, making the handle lift up the napkin in a very eerie way!

4 Grip the prongs through the napkin with one hand and use both hands to pull the napkin slowly towards you, letting the fork fall into your lap. Throw the napkin onto the table to show that it is empty!

★ **STAR TIPS** ★
Put a tablecloth on the table so that the fork does not make a sound when it is laid down.

DRACULA'S FANGS

Try as you might you cannot be rid of Dracula's third fang!

PREPARATION

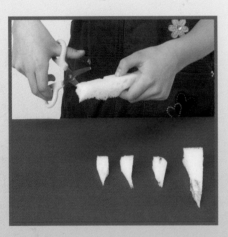

PERFORMANCE

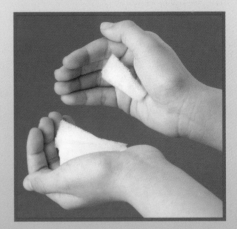

1 Carefully cut five fang shapes from the sponge – four about 3cm long, and one about 6cm long.

2 Put the big fang in your right pocket and place three of the small fangs on a table. Keep the final small fang secretly in your right hand.

1 Tell your audience that you have three of Dracula's fangs on the table, which is very dangerous so you will try to get rid of one of them. With one small fang still hidden in your right hand, pick up two of the fangs on the table, then place all three in your left hand and close it tight.

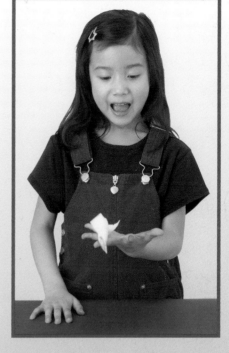

2 Pick up the last fang from the table and pretend to put it in your pocket but secretly keep it in your right hand. Open your left hand to reveal three fangs and tip them onto the table.

4 Open your left hand and let the three fangs fall onto the table again. With the big fang still in your right hand, pick up one fang from the table and put them both into your left hand. Now put the two remaining fangs in your pocket and open your left hand again so the big fang and the small fang jump out!

3 Repeat step 1 so you are left with three fangs in your closed left hand again. Pick up the last fang on the table with your right hand and this time do put it in your pocket but exchange it for the big fang already there, keeping it hidden in your right hand.

★ **STAR TIPS** ★
You can use a red pen to draw trickles of blood on the tips of the fangs.

Vanishing Eyeball

It is hard to keep an eye on this eye when it vanishes from a box!

PREPARATION

1 Use the pens to make the ping-pong ball look like an eyeball – add lots of red lines to make it look bloodshot!

PERFORMANCE

2 Open out the handkerchief and place the eyeball on it near one edge. Cut a piece of thread to reach from the centre of the handkerchief to the eyeball. Use the sticky tape to stick one end to the middle of the cloth and the other to the back of the eyeball.

3 Place the ball in the middle of the handkerchief, making sure that the thread is hidden underneath. Gather the corners of the handkerchief up to make a bag and put the whole thing in the box.

1 Put the box on a table and lift out the handkerchief by the corners saying that there is something inside that you are trying to keep an eye on. Place the handkerchief in your left hand and unfold it to show the eyeball inside.

2 Pick up the eyeball and show it to the audience, making sure the thread is not seen.

3 Put the eyeball back in the handkerchief and put it in the box with the handkerchief covering it.

4 Spread out the handkerchief so it covers the box entirely, then wave your hand over the box and pick up the handkerchief by one corner, lifting it right off the box to reveal that the eyeball has disappeared!

Dead Man's Finger

What's inside the matchbox? It looks like . . .
no, it can't be! Can it?

WHAT YOU NEED
- An empty matchbox
- Scissors
- Glue
- Cotton wool

PREPARATION

2 Stick some cotton wool around the edges of the hole, place another piece of cotton wool loosely over the top and slide the drawer back into the matchbox sleeve.

PERFORMANCE

1 Remove the drawer from the matchbox and carefully cut a slot in the bottom that is big enough for you to push your finger through so that it lies flat.

1 Bring out the matchbox and say that you have a dead man's finger inside. Carefully push the drawer out, place the sleeve to one side and put the drawer in your left hand.

2 Keep your right hand over the top of the drawer and secretly curl your left middle finger into the slot, underneath the loose piece of cotton wool.

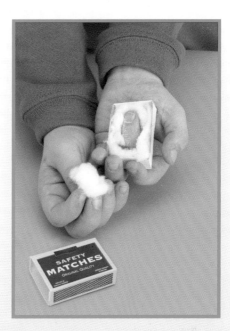

3 Once your finger is in position use your right hand to lift off the loose cotton wool and reveal the finger inside – it looks really realistic!

★ **STAR TIPS** ★

When you lift off the loose cotton wool keep your right hand in front of your left hand to cover up your fingertips and knuckle.

Phantom Coin

Amaze your friends with the phantom coin – it can move through solid walls!

WHAT YOU NEED
- A pack of cards in its box
- Nail scissors or a craft knife
- Two 10p coins

PREPARATION

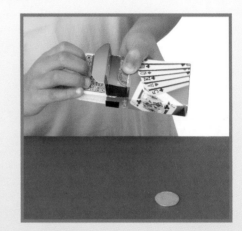

2 Slide the edge of one of the coins into the slit and hold the coin in place while you put the cards back.

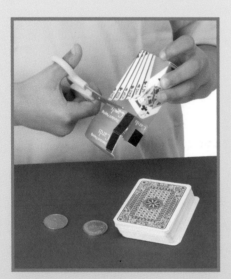

1 Remove the cards from the box and ask an adult to help you cut a slit in the back of the box. It should be 35mm wide and near one end.

PERFORMANCE

1 Pick up the box of cards in your left hand with your thumb at the back and your fingers at the front. Your fingers will cover the coin in the slit.

2 Open the box with your right hand, slide the cards out and put them down to one side. Shake the box while holding the coin in place so that the box sounds empty and close the lid of the box.

3 Show the other coin and tell the audience that it is a phantom coin because it can spirit itself through the walls of the box. Put the coin in your pocket with your right hand then show that your hand is empty.

4 Pretend to watch the phantom coin as it flies from your pocket to the box, then use your left fingers to secretly push the coin through the slit and into the box. Shake the box so it rattles and tip out the coin!

★ **STAR TIPS** ★
If you remove a few cards from the pack it will be easier to fit them in the box with the coin.

BOYS AND GHOULS

Two boys try to trap a ghoul but somehow it escapes!

PREPARATION

WHAT YOU NEED
- Three pieces of card
- A pen
- A hole punch
- A piece of thin string 20cm long

I Draw a picture of a boy on two of the cards and a creepy ghoul on the other. Put the cards in a neat pile and use the hole punch to make a hole 5mm from the top edge of the cards.

PERFORMANCE

I Show the cards to your audience and explain that the boys will tie up the ghoul so it cannot escape. Then hold the cards face down in a pile in your left hand with the ghoul card at the bottom and your left palm covering the back half of the cards.

2 Use your right fingertips to push the bottom card back a little so that the top edge of the card slides behind the holes in the other two cards.

4 Now hold the ends of the string together in your right hand and grip the cards in your left. Give a sharp tug on the string and the boys will fly out of your hand on the string but the ghoul will escape and stay in your hand!

3 Thread the string through the holes in the pile of cards and use your right hand to secretly push the bottom card back into place so all three cards are lined up.

★ **STAR TIPS** ★
You can ask a spectator to examine the string to distract your audience while you push the ghoul card back.

Wizards' Hats

The wizards' hats look empty, but you might get a shock when you look underneath!

WHAT YOU NEED
- Three pieces of card 10cm x 10cm
- Sticky tape
- Scissors
- A small rubber eyeball

PREPARATION

2 Cut off the wide end of the cone so that it will stand up on this end. The wide end of the cone should be big enough for the eyeball to fit snugly inside.

1 Hold two opposite corners of a piece of card together and make a small crease at the top corner fold. Now you can roll the card into a cone using the crease. Overlap the edges so that the cone is solid and stick it down with sticky tape.

3 Do this with all three pieces of card to make your wizards' hats. Stack the hats loosely on top of each other on a table and place the eyeball underneath.

PERFORMANCE

1 Pick up the stack of hats, squeezing the sides slightly so that you secretly pick up the eyeball as well. Place the stack in your left hand with your fingers curled around it.

3 Quickly take back the first hat and place it back in your left hand to cover the eyeball. Then take back the other hats and stack them on top. Pick up the stack with the eyeball inside and place it on the table.

2 Slide off the top hat and ask a spectator to examine it. Then lift off the second hat and do the same. Finally lift off the last hat, making sure your left fingers hide the eyeball.

★ STAR TIPS ★

You can decorate the hats to make them look spookier! Use sticky stars and glitter or draw spiders in webs! If you cannot find a rubber eyeball the right size you can make one by drawing an eye on a plain ball as in the Vanishing Eyeball trick on page 30.

4 Snap your fingers over the top and ask a spectator to remove the hats – they will get a shock when they find the eyeball looking up at them!

SPOOKY SPELL

Mix up a spooky spell in your cauldron!

PREPARATION

1 Write one of these words on each of the cards: WORM, RAT, MAN, SPIDER, EYE, WITCH, BLOOD, BAT, FROG, SLIME. Arrange the cards in this order face down so that WORM is at the bottom and SLIME is at the top.

PERFORMANCE

2 On the piece of paper, write the following words in this order: BAT, EYE, SLIME, WORM, FROG, RAT, BLOOD. This is your list of ingredients.

1 Show your list and tell the audience you are about to weave a spell. Hold the pile in your left hand and explain that the cards will spell out the ingredients. Start with the first word on your list – BAT. For each letter take a card from the top of the pile and put it at the bottom. As you spell out the last letter, 'T', turn the card face up to show that it says BAT and place it on the table.

2 Do the same for EYE, putting the 'E' and 'Y' cards on the bottom of the pile and turning over the last card to reveal 'EYE'. Then place that card with the 'BAT' card on the table. Now spell out SLIME in the same way and add that card to the table.

3 Ask a spectator to try it, giving them the pile of cards and the next ingredient – WORM. It looks easy, but when they turn over the 'M' card it says SPIDER! Take the pile back and put 'SPIDER' back on top. Spell out WORM and you will reveal 'WORM'. Add that card to the table.

★ **STAR TIPS** ★
You can make your trick look snazzier by drawing pictures on the cards to represent the ingredients. You can illustrate your list of ingredients as well with clues to remind you which cards your helper needs to spell out.

4 Ask the spectator to try again. When they try the next word – FROG – they will end up with 'SPIDER' again! Take the cards back, putting 'SPIDER' back on top. Spell FROG and place that on the table.

5 Ask the spectator to have a final try with RAT. They will turn over 'SPIDER' yet again! Take the cards back, putting 'SPIDER' back on top, spell RAT and add that to the table.

6 Now all the ingredients are in the cauldron, but you need someone to make the spell work. Turn over the top card to reveal a WITCH! But what will the spell create? Turn over the next card to show 'SPIDER' and the last card to reveal 'MAN'. The witch will make Spiderman!

The Hair of a Witch

Witch's hair is indestructible – and you can prove it!

PREPARATION

1 Cut the shoelace into two lengths – one 60cm long, the other 5cm long.

2 Fold the long piece in half and put it on a table. Fold the small piece in half and hold it in your left hand between your thumb and your first two fingers with the ends pointing down.

PERFORMANCE

1 Pick up the long piece of lace with your right hand and tell the audience that it is a strand of witch's hair, which is impossible to destroy.

2 Place the centre loop in your left hand and hold it below the small piece of lace hidden there. At the same time move the small piece of lace up so that the loop clearly shows over your fingers.

3 Take the scissors and carefully cut the top off this loop, then trim away the small piece of lace bit by bit and scatter them on the floor, so that the only thing left in your hand is the long piece.

★ **STAR TIPS** ★

The tricky bit here is to put the long piece of lace in your hand and move the other piece up at the same time. Practise this until you are sure it looks natural.

4 Explain that even though you have clearly cut it, witch's hair can mend itself. Slowly pull out the long piece of lace to reveal that it is still in one piece!

genie in a bottle

The genie in this bottle doesn't like intruders!

PREPARATION

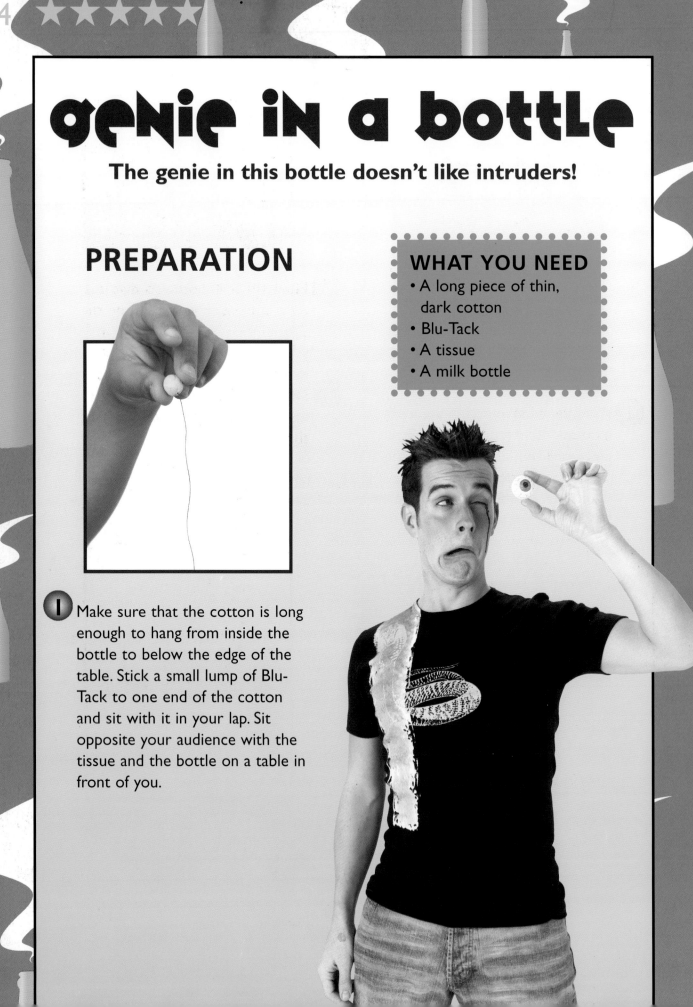

1 Make sure that the cotton is long enough to hang from inside the bottle to below the edge of the table. Stick a small lump of Blu-Tack to one end of the cotton and sit with it in your lap. Sit opposite your audience with the tissue and the bottle on a table in front of you.

PERFORMANCE

1 Ask a member of the audience to examine the bottle and the tissue and see if they can spot the genie inside the bottle. Tell them that you can prove he really is there.

2 Ask another spectator to pass you the tissue and at the same time secretly take the Blu-Tack end of the cotton in your right hand on your lap. Pick up the tissue, put it in your right hand and bunch it up into a ball with the Blu-Tack hidden inside.

3 Move the milk bottle so that it is right in front of you and drop the tissue inside. Take the cotton in your right hand under the table and explain that the genie does not like having things put into his bottle so he may try to get rid of the tissue.

4 Slowly pull on the cotton in your lap a few times. The tissue will jump up and down in the bottle as if the genie is trying to throw it out!

★ **STAR TIPS** ★
Before you start this trick make sure that you are wearing a top the same colour as the thread. If you do this, the thread will not be very obvious when you drop the tissue into the bottle.

Haunted Halloween!

Halloween is a time for ghostly goings-on so the tricks in this book are perfect for a creepy, Halloween magic show. But do you know how Halloween began?

Halloween dates back to the Celts, 2,000 years ago. Their year was split into two seasons – the growing season and the winter season – the life and death of the year. The winter season was known as Samhain (pronounced sow-in) and started on the 1st November.

The Celts believed that on the first night of Samhain the boundaries between the worlds of the living and the dead were blurred and the spirits of those who had died that year returned.

Their relatives hollowed out turnips to carry the spirits back. But, there were other, nastier spirits around too, so people carved scary faces into the turnips to chase them away. To protect themselves they painted their faces and wore strange costumes. Nowadays we still carve pumpkins and wear scary costumes at Halloween.

The Celts also believed in faeries – mischievous creatures who played tricks on humans. On the first night of Samhain faeries were said to disguise themselves as beggars and knock at doors asking for gifts.

It was believed that those who gave them food were rewarded with good luck, but those who refused would regret it! Today children go trick-or-treating at Halloween like the faeries.

Bonfires also played a big part in Samhain – the Celts would light a giant bonfire in the main square of the town. Some believed they could look into the fire and see the future. Bonfires are no longer a part of Halloween in England – now we remember Guy Fawkes' gunpowder plot with bonfires and fireworks on the 5th November.

Halloween is now a fun time for dressing up, trick-or-treating and telling spooky stories – it has come a long way from the night of the dead in which the Celts believed, but you can still see their customs in our parties. Why not really spook your friends this Halloween with some of the tricks in this book – all in the name of tradition!

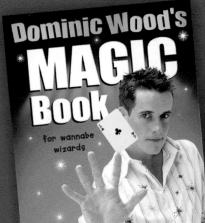

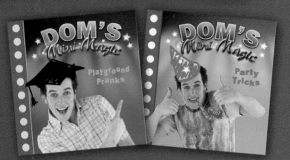